POCKETGUIDE SERIES

BASIC CRIME SCENE INVESTIGATION

LOU SAVELLI

43-08 162nd S
www.Loosele

D1303351

ISBN 1-889031-99-2

Cover design by *Sans Serif, Inc.* Saline, Michigan

About the Pocketguide Series

Law Enforcement Officers (LEOs) are faced with ever-changing trends and issues and have little time to spend on in-depth research and reference. The Pocketguide series of books have been created to assist law enforcement officers in the endeavor to remain up-to-date on these ever-changing trends. The Pocketguide series provides *to the point* reference information on contemporary important issues.

We at CTS Associates Incorporated, creators of the Pocketguide series, have painstakingly researched and developed the following valuable and useful information.

The Pocketguide books, as you will see, will provide a current, quick and easy-to-use, pocket-sized tool that was written in an easy to read style. When hundreds of pages of information or volumes of material are not feasible to carry around and time does not permit its study, the Pocketguide books will fill that void and provide the right reference.

Please enjoy this useful pocket-sized book and keep in mind that we at CTS Associates Incorporated wish you safety and efficiency in your endeavor to fight the scourge of crime in our society.

Call Toll-Free for other Recent Editions to the
Pocketguide Series and a **_Free_** catalog.

(800) 647-5547
Looseleaf Law Publications, Inc.
Flushing, NY
www.looseleaflaw.com

About the Author

Lou Savelli, is a 23-year veteran of law enforcement. He has spent his last 21 years with the NYPD and has conducted countless criminal investigations as a proactive plainclothes street cop, a detective, and a detective squad commander. He boasts that he has spent his entire career on the streets in pursuit of criminals and fighting crime because he loves it. He says that he learned more about crime-fighting from the criminals on the streets than he did from any Police Academy he attended.

While he has spent many years, in his off-duty time, working toward a continuing education at John Jay College of Criminal Justice and the State University of New York, he feels the education he received from the streets of New York City, the men and women of the NYPD and the other agencies he has worked alongside, the great bosses he has worked under, and the street smarts he has gained, enabled him to survive and thrive as a crime fighter.

Twice awarded as Supervisor of the Year, he was recognized by then Police Commissioner William Bratton as one of NYPD's most effective leaders of all ranks (out of 10,000 supervisors) and the NYPD's first supervisor highlighted in the Leadership Newsletter for his outstanding leadership role in his highly successful Anti-Crime Unit.

In 1996, Lou Savelli created and commanded NYPD's first street gang unit called CAGE (Citywide Anti-Gang Enforcement Unit), which was awarded the National Gang

Crime Research Center's award for The Most Effective Gang Unit in the United States. Since then, several gang units across the US and Canada have modeled themselves after the proactive methods used by the CAGE Unit.

He is the Vice President, and cofounder, of the East Coast Gang Investigators Association and one of the original members of the International Counter Terrorism Officers' Association. He has been a career-long member of dozens of other law enforcement associations but credits the Police Writers' Association with encouraging him to write.

Not only has he been a player in the game of fighting crime, on duty and off, but says he is also a student of it. He said, *"When you think you know all there is about catching criminals and preventing crime, you probably will get shot by a perp that day! There is always more to learn!"* According to Lou, the best advice he ever received was from his father, deceased since 1979, when he said: *"Always keep seeking knowledge because when you stop learning, you're dead!"*

He has authored four other law enforcement books, written several published short stories, and numerous articles, and is also the Vice President in charge of Operations for CTS Associates Incorporated, a Law Enforcement Consulting and Training company.

As a Patrol and Detective Supervisor for NYPD for over thirteen years, and a veteran of hundreds of crime scenes, Lou Savelli learned a great deal about Crime Scene Investigation. This Pocketguide is a brief, but thorough, manual for basic crime scene investigation.

Table of Contents

Introduction

This ***Pocketguide to Crime Scene Investigation*** was created to be a handy pocket reference and procedural guide to be utilized during any crime scene. It is intended to be useful to any law enforcement officer or related professional who may become involved in the security, maintenance, investigation, or documenting of a crime scene. It is not intended to replace departmental procedures or local laws pertaining to crime scenes and crime scene investigations. Law enforcement officers can refer to this Pocketguide prior to responding to the scene of a crime, after establishing a crime scene or during the investigation of a crime scene, to insure the proper steps of crime scene investigation.

This Pocketguide, and its procedures, can be used by many law enforcement officers that are involved in the establishment and investigation of crime scenes and searching crime scenes. These crime scenes may be spur of the moment, accidental or a result of law enforcement actions. This Pocketguide can be useful to:

- ✓ Patrol Officers
- ✓ Detectives
- ✓ Supervisors
- ✓ Narcotics Agents

- ✓ Tactical Officers
- ✓ Vice Investigators
- ✓ Corrections Officers
- ✓ Parole Officers
- ✓ Probation Officers
- ✓ Security Professionals
- ✓ Federal Agents
- ✓ Military Police

The information, definitions, techniques and methods detailed in the *Pocketguide to Crime Scene Investigation* have been compiled from a variety of trusted sources. The information, definitions, techniques and methods are merely suggestions and reminders to maintain an organized and efficient manner of crime scene investigation. At no time do the writers and researchers of this work claim that it should replace departmental procedures and guidelines. Additionally, those legal guidelines existing in each jurisdiction must prevail for the legality of one's actions and the admissibility of collected evidence at a crime scene.

What is a Crime Scene?

A crime scene, basically defined, is any physical location in which a crime has occurred or is suspected of having occurred. Such locations will require preservation, documentation and investigation to further determine if a crime has occurred or to assist in solving a crime and/or apprehending a perpetrator of a crime. Crime scenes include, but are not limited to, homicide scenes, suicide scenes, auto accident scenes, burglary scenes, robbery scenes, sexual assault scenes, search warrant locations or any place where a crime has just occurred.

Crimes and crime scenes can happen at any time at any location. An organized, systematic method of crime scene investigation is necessary to gather as much information and evidence as possible. Placing an organized and systematic method of crime scene investigation into operation will greatly increase the solvability of crime.

Responding to the Crime Scene

Upon receiving information that a crime has occurred and you are responding to a crime scene or potential crime scene, obtain as much information as possible from the person or dispatcher directing, or requesting, your response. Write the information in your notepad. The following information will be of the utmost importance to your initial response to the crime scene:

- The nature of the crime or investigation
- Are there any victims?
- Are the victims injured or likely to die?
- Has anyone been taken to the hospital?
- Are there any perpetrators?
- Are they on the scene?
- In custody?
- What are the perpetrators' descriptions, direction of flight, etc...?
- Are there any witnesses?
- Who is the first officer on the scene?
- Who called the police (the 911 call)?
- Time of first information (or 911 call)
- Were there any previous calls at this location?

Arrival to the Crime Scene

Upon arrival to the crime scene, make a notation in your notepad of the following information:

- Date and time of arrival
- Address of the scene and cross streets
- First/Primary officer's name and badge number (if you are not the first officer on the scene)
- Lighting and weather conditions
- General description of the scene and building addresses
- Vehicles on the scene
- Nearby bus or train stops or routes
- Nearby stores or other businesses (if open or closed)
- Type and amount of non-law enforcement persons on scene
- Law enforcement personnel on the scene and vehicle numbers
- Other official personnel on the scene and vehicle numbers

Make contact with the primary (first) officer on the scene or the officer who is preserving the scene and record his/her pedigree information, telephone number, next tour of duty, and record his/her statements. Determine that proper preservation of the crime scene has occurred, and if it has not, establish the proper crime scene immediately.

Establishing and Securing a Crime Scene

If you are the primary officer or it is necessary for you to establish a safe and secure crime scene, the following steps must be taken immediately:

- Maintain your own safety, victims and others
- If necessary, render first aid to victims
- Determine if perpetrators are present and apprehend/detain perpetrators/suspects, if possible
- Issue a description and flight information of perpetrator(s) if known
- Quickly and efficiently, clear the largest area possible
- If multiple crime scenes, try to clear an area encompassing all scenes
- Expeditiously, cordon off the area with crime scene tape or rope
- Make a quick evaluation of the scene
- Detain witnesses, potential witnesses and suspects
- Separate witnesses
- Identify person who first contacted the police
- When possible, make a notation in your notepad of the following information:

  ✓ Date and time of arrival

- ✓ Address of the scene
- ✓ Information that led you to the scene
- ✓ Any information you received from others (official or not)
- ✓ Victim information
- ✓ Perpetrator information
- ✓ Lighting conditions
- ✓ Description of the scene & building addresses
- ✓ Vehicles on the scene
- ✓ Nearby bus or train stops or route
- ✓ Nearby stores or other businesses
- ✓ Type and amount of non-law enforcement personnel on the scene
- ✓ Law enforcement personnel on the scene and vehicle numbers
- ✓ Weather conditions

- Keep ALL unauthorized persons OUT of the crime scene
- Contact and utilize back-up when necessary to maintain safety and accomplish required duties
- Maintain a chronological log and take notes of activity and authorized persons arriving to the crime scene. Write down the name, rank, agency, badge or serial number, purpose of entry to scene, vehicle number

Conducting a Canvass

Canvassing is done for witnesses, suspects, and sometimes, additional victims of a crime. It can be done door-to-door or with people on the street. Any building, street corner, or location with someone who may have information about the crime should be included in your canvass. Canvassing should include the surrounding area of a crime scene, possible escape routes from the scene and potential hiding places for suspects. The scope and time of the canvass should be determined by considering conditions and factors such as the type of crime, time of occurrence, time of day of canvass and weather conditions. The canvass interview should be done in a brief manner at each location to cover as much area as possible and be conducted within a reasonable proximity of the crime scene or possible escape routes. When conducting the canvass, the officer should:

▶ State his/her name, rank, agency

▶ Be polite and interested

▶ Purpose for the interview

▶ Issue a telephone number to call if information arises at a later date

In the brief canvass interview, the officer conducting the canvass should note the following information in his/her notepad:

▶ Date and Time of Interview

▶ Address, apartment number

▶ Name of person interviewed (each person spoken to)

▶ Pedigree information of person (Date of Birth, Description, etc…)

▶ Telephone number of person interviewed

▶ Takes Notes of the information obtained, or if no information was obtained, or if there was no answer at the location

▶ If others residing in location are not home at the time of the initial canvass, ascertain when and how to contact them when canvassing further

Note: When conducting the canvass, keep in mind that people will feel more comfortable when approached from a standpoint of confidentiality and tend to speak more freely in a confidential setting. When safe, and feasible, try to request to enter the person's home to establish confidentiality and speak in a tone lending itself to confidentiality.

Suggested Canvass Proximity

(X = Crime Scene Site)

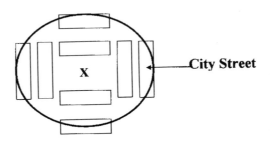

Note: When organizing a canvass, consider the following acronym that represents the determining factors of where and when a canvass should be conducted:

R. A. T. T.

Reasonableness
Area
Time of Day
Time of Crime

Reasonableness should be used to determine how far a canvass should reach, how long the duration of the canvass should be, and who should be approached during a canvass. It is reasonable to canvass at a nearby day care center but it is not reasonable to question the children.

Area is determined by the proximity of the crime scene in which a person or device (closed circuit cameras) could potentially have information about the crime. It would be reasonable to canvass within a street or two surrounding the crime scene in a densely populated urban neighborhood but it wouldn't be reasonable to canvass five streets away.

Time of Day of the canvass will be chosen for the highest degree of efficiency of the canvass. A canvass should be conducted during the time of day that would facilitate positive results.

Time of the Crime will determine who will be interviewed as part of the canvass that may have valuable information about the crime and could have possibly been exposed to the crime in some manner.

Interviewing Witnesses at a Crime Scene

Interviewing witnesses at a crime scene should be done as quickly as possible. Don't leave witnesses milling around to exchange or hear stories that may taint their account of what had occurred. Also, witnesses that are unattended and on their own, leave a great potential for witness intimidation and witness disappearing.

When you are the *first officer* on the scene and not the investigating officer, follow these simple rules:

1. Obtain witness pedigree information first, in case they disappear

2. Keep witnesses separated

3. Show an interest in the witnesses

4. Try to keep an eye on witnesses

5. Avoid talking about the crime in front of witnesses

6. Take notes about what the witness says that is pertinent to this crime

If you are the investigator responsible for the interview of witnesses, you should:

1. Interview the first officer prior to the witnesses to determine which witness should be interviewed first

2. Introduce yourself to the witnesses

3. State your name, authority and purpose

4. Obtain the witnesses' pedigree information first, in case they disappear

5. Keep witnesses separated and interview away from other witnesses

6. Show an interest in the witnesses

7. Avoid talking about the crime in front of the witnesses

8. Take notes of witness statements, with special notice of details, descriptions and times

9. Give the witness an idea of what to expect during the follow-up investigation (Is he needed for ID process, further interview, etc…)

10. Before completing the interview, leave your phone number with the witness and direct the witness to contact you with any further information

REMEMBER: *Witnesses are interviewed and suspects are interrogated.*

Initial Photographing of the Crime Scene

Upon Arrival to a Crime Scene, when possible, photograph or ensure photographing of the entire scene prior to entering the area. Should you have access to a video camera, use it! The video camera has many uses. Photography/Video should capture as much as possible of the overall crime scene.

The initial photograph (or video) should include the following:

- The overall scene
- Victims
- Onlookers
- Witnesses
- Buildings
- Vehicles

- Street signs
- Fixed objects
- Lighting source
- Weather (if applicable)
- Pedestrian traffic

Do your best to photograph the entire scene as a broad area. Next, take a closer view, and conclude with a close-up view. When possible, try to utilize measurements such as rulers, yardsticks or known-scale items. Take a photograph of significant evidence prior to the evidence being manipulated, moved, or its removal. Crime scene and evidence photos should be an accurate and efficient depiction of the crime scene. Photos should be able to include the evidence and its significance to the crime scene. For example, when photographing a crowbar near the doorway of a burglary scene, the crowbar should be photographed with the doorway in the picture.

If available, a video camera is preferable. A video camera, when used properly, can capture the scene in a more realistic view. Still photos can easily be rendered from the video footage. The investigator may even talk-over the video to explain the scene. In all cases, the investigator should prepare a rough sketch of the scene to back-up and assist in explaining your crime scene photos or video.

Preliminary Crime Scene *Walk-through*

The preliminary walk-through should be conducted prior to commencing the actual search for evidence and clues. The walk-through is a physical survey of the entire crime scene and surrounding area to evaluate the crime scene, evaluate potential evidence, determine if the crime scene will be expanded or narrowed, determine the appropriate search pattern to utilize, determine the appropriate equipment needed for the actual search, and to familiarize yourself with the crime scene. The walk-through should be concluded with a brief written narrative report describing the crime scene.

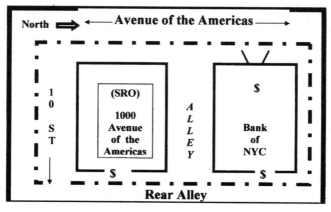

Example of Notes:

1010 Avenue of the Americas, Bank of New York City, Bank Burglary, Upon arrival, 0230 hours, met with first officer Donald Devito, badge # 987, Post 19, who responded at 0200 hours, to a 911 call of a bank alarm/burglary in progress. When he arrived, with back-up officer Bramson, Post 18, they found the bank had been burglarized and no suspects were on the scene. A bag of money was found near the broken front glass door. He secured the scene. Photographed the front of the scene and interior. Conducted walk-through of the scene and the surrounding buildings and discovered several 20 dollar bills in the rear alley and near the adjacent SRO complex (rear door) next door (1000 Ave. of Americas). Expanded the crime scene to the area surrounding the bank and SRO.

Searching the Crime Scene

The purpose of searching the crime scene is to recover evidence, develop a feel for the crime and the scene, and better understand the victim's actions. In order to efficiently search the crime scene, a proven method should be utilized. There are several proven and accepted methods of searching a crime scene. The method chosen should be determined by considering the following uniqueness of the crime scene: freshness, size, location, diverseness, complexity and resources.

Such crime scene search methods are:

1. Strip Method
2. Spiral Method
3. Wheel Method
4. Grid Method
5. Zone Method

Strip Method

The Strip Method is a suggested method when the area to be searched is large and open. This method can be conducted by a single investigator or multiple investigators. It is a quick method of searching a crime scene.

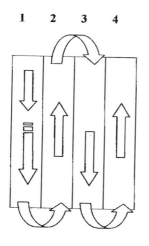

In the strip method, one or more investigators can search the crime scene. When more than one investigator is available to search, the second investigator can start on section 2 and continue on section 4

Spiral Method

The Spiral Method is utilized in a circular search pattern around the crime scene. Depending upon where the investigator begins the search, at the perimeter or at the center, he/she either gradually widens the search toward the perimeter of the crime scene or gradually narrows the search toward the center of the crime scene.

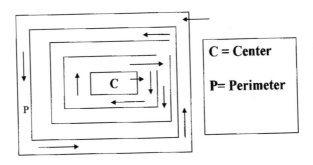

C = Center

P= Perimeter

Wheel Method

In the wheel method, investigators will begin at the center of the crime scene and move outward, searching the areas they pass.

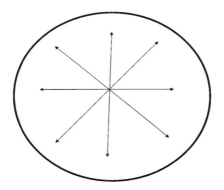

Grid Method

The investigator(s) search in the direction of the grids until they reach the end of the grid row. At the end of the row, the investigator(s) searches in an adjacent parallel direction slightly overlapping the area already covered to insure the most efficient method of evidence recovery. With two or more investigators, the same area is covered twice.

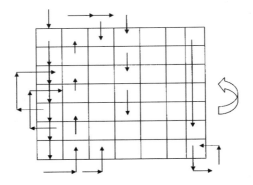

Zone Method

The Zone Method calls for the search area to be divided into sectors, which will be numbered and searched by an individual investigator or several investigators. Each number is assigned an investigator to search the number of the sector they are assigned.

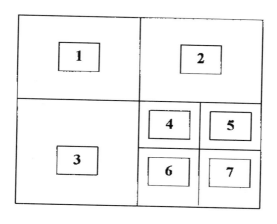

Documenting the Crime Scene

The best and most likely the easiest way to document the crime scene is to record everything possible in your investigators or patrol officer's notepad or memo book.

Document the following:

- ✓ Date
- ✓ Time
- ✓ Crime Suspected
- ✓ Dispatch Information
- ✓ First Officer's Information
- ✓ Your notes
- ✓ Witness Information
- ✓ Suspect Information
- ✓ Authorized and Unauthorized Persons on the scene
- ✓ If, When and What Photographs were taken
- ✓ Sketches
- ✓ Evidence
- ✓ Custody of Evidence
- ✓ Any other Investigative measures and any other pertinent information can be documented in your notepad

O   O   O

7/1/02, 1400 hours, 911 call of Homicide at 1400 Broadway, Room 237. Apparent gunshot victim. Uniform Officers on scene. No suspect information. One witness on scene. 1415 hours arrived. Observed a white plastic bag stuffed in the incinerator down the hall from the victim's apartment. (Check That Out!)

1416 hours, Met with First Officer PO John Smith, badge #876, 13th Precinct, Sector Adam. He states the victim's name is Ahmed Mohammad, 35, who lives alone. The landlord, Mr. Stein, on scene, found the body.

1420 hours, interviewed Paramedic Jane Jones #45 and Bob Thompson #77 who pronounced DOA at 1345 hours.

1425 hours, interviewed landlord William Stein, 1400 Broadway, Room 122, Tel #555-1212, who discovered the body. Mr. Stein states: "Mr. Mohammad lives alone and has no known relatives in the US. He found the door open at approximately 1:00 pm when he came by to pick up the rent. He entered and found the victim unconscious and bleeding. He called 911."

Rough Crime Scene Sketch

As soon as the investigator arrives on the scene, after the initial photographs are taken, a rough sketch should be prepared with important information depicted. The rough sketch is an investigator's insurance and memory of the crime scene in its purest form (the way it was when the investigator arrived). In case another investigator or the Medical Examiner moves the victim's body or a piece of evidence, the rough sketch will be able to show the difference.

The sketch of the scene should show the following information:

- ✓ Location of the body (if applicable)

- ✓ Point of entry (if known)

- ✓ Apparent Evidence such as weapons, drugs

- ✓ Rendering of doors and windows (open, closed, ajar)

- ✓ The state of time sensitive (ice cubes, burning cigarettes, stove, etc..)

Rough Sketch:

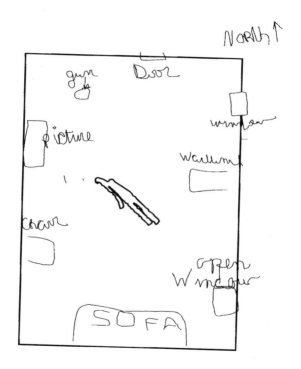

North ↑

gun

Door

window

picture

wall unit

chair

open window

SOFA

Collection and Documentation of Evidence

Evidence can be collected at a crime scene, from the body of the victim, from the person of a suspect, or from other locations and persons that are uncovered pursuant to an investigation. Proper collection and documentation of evidence will greatly increase the chances of the evidence being admitted into court proceedings. When attempting to collect evidence, the investigator must keep the following questions in mind:

- ✓ What evidence links the victim with the crime scene?

- ✓ What evidence links the perpetrator with the crime scene?

- ✓ What evidence links the perpetrator to the victim?

While collecting evidence at a crime scene, from a victim, from a suspect or from other persons or locations, the investigator must efficiently catalog the evidence to properly document evidence collection. A crime scene evidence log may be created, a catalog sheet of evidence, or simply a list of evidence in the investigator's notebook can suffice. When logging the evidence, the investigator should list the following information:

- Description of Evidence

- Owner of Evidence (if known)

- Location of evidence recovery

- Date and Time of recovery

- Name of person recovering

- Persons present during recovery

- Name of person taking custody (if custody is passed on)

- Purpose of evidence recovery

- Type of examination (if any) requested

- Who and where examination should be conducted

- Evidence collection item number

- Evidence Invoice number and package/bag/ envelope number

Final Crime Scene Sketch

The crime scene sketch should be a simple drawing of the crime scene that details as much about the scene as possible. It can be based on the Rough Sketch that is made upon arrival to the scene. The sketch should be prepared at the scene so the investigator can be as accurate as possible. This sketch will be the basis for the final crime scene sketch created later, if possible, in a professional manner. It can serve as a way to refresh the investigator's memory later on in the investigation, or in court. It may be utilized to refresh the memory of witnesses and cooperating suspects. The sketch can show dimensions and positioning that may not be properly depicted in the crime scene photographs.

The crime scene sketch should include:

- ✓ Title of Sketch with Investigator and Case Information:
  - Date
  - Investigator's Name, Rank, Badge Number
  - Sketch prepared by, if different than the primary investigator
  - Crime
  - Complaint Number
  - Investigator's/Detective Case Number
  - Address

- ✓ Position of the body (if a homicide)

- ✓ Fixed objects (furniture, walls, doors, etc.)

- ✓ Evidence locations

- ✓ Blood trails, splatters, drops

- ✓ Points of entry

- ✓ Measurements (if not to scale, list it prominently)

- ✓ North, South, East, West

- ✓ Sketch Legend with evidence (numbered) recovered

There are several types of crime scene sketches utilized by investigators. Each sketch method is based on the diversity, complexity, and availability of details at the crime scene. One or more crime scene sketches may be utilized to efficiently document the scene.

The various types of crime scene sketches are illustrated on the following pages.

Cross Projection Sketch: This type of sketch shows a view from above with the walls folded down.

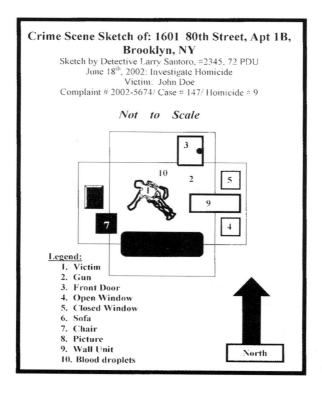

Crime Scene Sketch of: 1601 80th Street, Apt 1B, Brooklyn, NY

Sketch by Detective Larry Santoro, #2345, 72 PDU
June 18th, 2002: Investigate Homicide
Victim: John Doe
Complaint # 2002-5674/ Case # 147/ Homicide # 9

Not to Scale

Legend:
1. Victim
2. Gun
3. Front Door
4. Open Window
5. Closed Window
6. Sofa
7. Chair
8. Picture
9. Wall Unit
10. Blood droplets

North

Base Line Sketch: Useful to sketch a large area with no boundaries, such as an outdoor area, the Baseline Sketch provides a point of reference

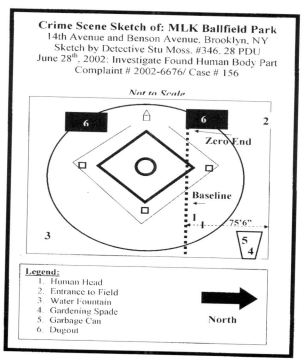

Crime Scene Sketch of: **MLK Ballfield Park**
14th Avenue and Benson Avenue, Brooklyn, NY
Sketch by Detective Stu Moss. #346. 28 PDU
June 28th, 2002: Investigate Found Human Body Part
Complaint # 2002-6676/ Case # 156

Not to Scale

6   6   2

Zero End

Baseline

1   75'6"

3   5   4

Legend:
1. Human Head
2. Entrance to Field
3. Water Fountain
4. Gardening Spade
5. Garbage Can
6. Dugout

North

Smooth Sketch: This is a sketch with a detailed legend and a dotted line to depict the path the perpetrator took through the crime scene.

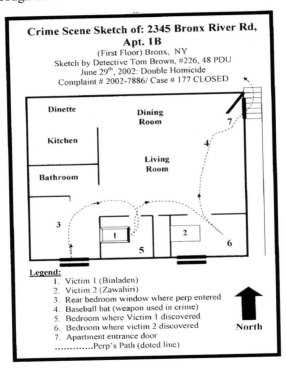

Crime Scene Sketch of: 2345 Bronx River Rd, Apt. 1B

(First Floor) Bronx, NY
Sketch by Detective Tom Brown, #226, 48 PDU
June 29th, 2002: Double Homicide
Complaint # 2002-7886/ Case # 177 CLOSED

Dinette

Dining Room

7

Kitchen

4

Living Room

Bathroom

3

1

2

5

6

Legend:
1. Victim 1 (Binladen)
2. Victim 2 (Zawahiri)
3. Rear bedroom window where perp entered
4. Baseball bat (weapon used in crime)
5. Bedroom where Victim 1 discovered
6. Bedroom where victim 2 discovered
7. Apartment entrance door
............Perp's Path (doted line)

North

Street Sketch: This sketch is used to depict the street as a crime scene or showing several locations and movements of a perpetrator(s).

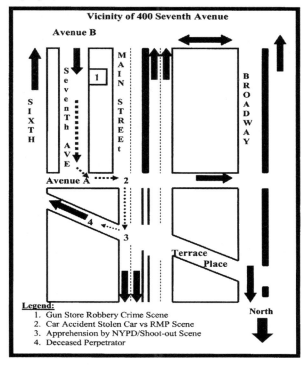

Vicinity of 400 Seventh Avenue

Legend:
1. Gun Store Robbery Crime Scene
2. Car Accident Stolen Car vs RMP Scene
3. Apprehension by NYPD/Shoot-out Scene
4. Deceased Perpetrator

Media and the Crime Scene

Members of the media should be barred from crime scenes at all times. Maintaining strict perimeters around the scene will insure that unauthorized persons, such as the media, will be kept out. First Officers who are not the responsible investigators for the crime should never discuss the crime or the crime scene with the media. Some media persons are relentless in asking questions and have a knack for extracting information from inexperienced officers.

While cooperating with the media is common practice for most law enforcement agencies, department policy, caution, and common sense should be your guide. Common sense should also guide you when identifying media persons at crime scenes. Counterfeit press credentials are quite common across the country. Examine EVERYONE'S press credentials at the scene of a crime.

Most press passes are issued by the local Police Department and can be revoked by that department if a violation of the rules and procedures is discovered.

Press Credentials

Jimmy Olson DOB: 2/12/65
Male, White, 180 lbs, 5'11"
Brown Hair, Brown Eyes
Daily Planet Newspaper, Inc.
Signature: *Jimmy Olson*

This Pass has been issued by the Police Department

Legal Issues and the Crime Scene

In order for collected evidence to be admissible in court, it must be legally seized. The rule in criminal investigations is to obtain a search warrant prior to conducting a search and potential seizure of evidence. In the case of a criminal investigation, when the victim and suspect share the residency or custody of the premises, a search warrant **must** be obtained prior to conducting a search. There are four exceptions, however, to the search warrant rule:

1. **Exigent Circumstances:** Exigent circumstances are when an emergency exists necessitating the investigator to disregard obtaining a search warrant. Exigent circumstances can be:

   - When the investigator fears evidence will be destroyed
   - When it will be unsafe to search later
   - When it is necessary to save lives or prevent harm

2. **Plain View:** Evidence or contraband in plain sight of a law enforcement officer can be seized without obtaining a warrant.

3. **Incidental to Arrest:** When a lawful arrest has been effected, an immediate search may be conducted of the person and the immediate reachable area surrounding or in his control.

4. **Consent:** A search warrant is not needed when the owner of a property gives consent to search.

Legal Admissibility
of Scientific Evidence

Most jurisdictions follow the Frye Rule for evaluating the admissibility of evidence. The Supreme Court ruled in *Frye v. United States* that when scientific evidence is introduced into a court of law, the evidence must have gained general acceptance in the scientific community. Like in the subject of DNA, it is generally used as scientific evidence and is accepted by the scientific community and therefore, will be admissible in a court of law.

In *Frye v. United States, F. 1013 at 1014 (D.C.Cir 1923)*. The court held:

"...Just when a scientific principal or discovery crosses the line between the experimental and demonstrable stages is difficult to define. Somewhere the evidential force of the principle must be recognized, and while courts will go a long way in admitting expert testimony deduced from a well-recognized scientific principle or discovery, the thing from which the deduction is made must be sufficiently established to have gained general acceptance in the particular field in which it belongs."

Closing the Crime Scene

After completing all necessary duties and responsibilities at a crime scene, or temporarily securing a crime scene until a later reasonable time, an investigator will have to properly close the crime scene. Closing a crime scene consists of securing the crime scene, posting notice on the crime scene, ability and legality to revisit the crime scene, and releasing the crime scene.

1. **Securing the Crime Scene:** Securing the crime scene, more likely than not, is not as simple as it sounds. Crime scene tape, "*Police Line Do Not Cross*" tape, or rope, may be insufficient to stop curiosity seekers, annoying landlords, the press, or even egomaniacal high-ranking officers from contaminating the crime scene or making an unauthorized visit. The crime scene should be secured by posting a conscientious uniformed officer at the front entrance of the scene. While you are still conducting a search of the crime scene, you may have to lock or barricade yourself in the scene to prevent visitors. When securing the crime scene for further search or investigation, be sure to post security personnel to maintain the integrity of the crime scene. The security must be an unbroken chain of security personnel and the crime scene must not be left unattended for a second.

2. **Posting Notice on the Crime Scene:** Posting a notice of *"Crime Scene, Do Not Enter!"* on the door and over the doorjamb will allow you to verify if an unauthorized person has entered the crime scene while you were away. If that happens, the integrity of the crime scene has been compromised. The use of a durable paper or plastic door seal will suffice in accomplishing this task.

> **Crime Scene**
>
> **Do Not Enter!**
>
> **By order of the Police Department**

3. **Ability and Legality to revisit the Crime Scene:** When it is necessary for an investigator to revisit the crime scene after leaving, the investigator must consider continuity of custody, contamination, and integrity of the crime scene that now exists as well as the legal issue of returning to a scene that has been abandoned. In many cases, when an officer has been posted continually on the crime scene since the investigators have left the scene and not yet released the scene, that crime scene is still considered in the custody of the law enforcement agency. When this custody has been broken for a period of time, the crime scene may have become contaminated and the integrity of the scene can no longer be trusted. Also, a search warrant may have to be issued by a judge to return to the scene. The

prosecutor or agency legal advisors should be conferred.

4. **Releasing the Crime Scene:** Releasing the scene from the investigator's control should only be done after the investigator carefully considers the answers to certain questions:

- Has the canvass been completed?

- Have all the witnesses been interviewed?

- Has the suspect in custody been fully questioned?

- Has an autopsy, if applicable, been completed?

- Has a thorough search been conducted and all obtainable evidence been collected?

- Have all crime scene duties been thoroughly completed?

- Has all equipment and notes belonging to the investigator been removed?

When the investigator can satisfy all these questions with a positive answer, then a crime scene can be released. The release must be made to a bonafide person responsible for the control of the location. Have that person sign your notepad or a pre-printed form accepting responsibility for the location and verifying the condition of the location.

Utilizing the Expertise of a
Forensic Specialist

It is sometimes necessary to bring in expertise from an outside unit or agency. The field of forensic science is so broad today that no agency will have every form of specialty service available from among its ranks. Forensic specialists may be utilized from private industry, the academic community, private scientific laboratories and others.

When choosing a forensic specialist, consider the competence and reliability of the specialist, the ability of the specialist to work at a scene within law enforcement guidelines, and the role and ability of the forensic specialist in presenting expert testimony in court. Forensic specialists should be identified prior to them being needed in a case. Current contact lists of forensic specialists should be maintained and meetings should be conducted with these specialists to determine the best protocol to conduct crime scene operations.

Keep in mind any profession can potentially provide expert assistance or testimony.

Example – The *master woodworker* can identify and validate the impressions made by a specific saw or cutting tool.

Following is a partial list of common Forensic Specialists that may be of assistance on certain criminal investigations or related crime scenes.

- Anthropologist
- Arson Expert
- Blood Pattern Analyst
- Bomb Technician
- Criminalist
- Cryptanalysis Expert
- Cult Expert
- DNA Specialist
- Engineer
- Entomologist
- Forensic Artist
- Gang Expert
- Handwriting Analyst
- Medical Examiner
- Narcotics Expert
- Occult Expert
- Odontologist

NOTES

Glossary of Terms and Definitions

Abrasion Collar: A circular perforation and blackening effect on the edges of the skin as a bullet passes through the skin.

Accelerant: A substance that is used to create and sometimes direct the spread of a fire. The most commonly used liquid accelerants include gasoline, lighter fluid, kerosene, and turpentine.

Accident Reconstruction: The use of physical evidence to build a theoretical model of a given crime or accident scene.

Acid Phosphatase: An enzyme found in the kidneys, semen, serum and prostate gland. It is useful as an indication of recent sexual intercourse.

Adipocere: A waxy soap-like substance formed during the decomposition of animal bodies buried in moist places.

Alibi: An explanation offered by a suspect or potential suspect explaining why he/she could not / did not commit the crime.

Anoxia: Total oxygen deprivation.

Ante mortem: Before death.

Anterior: The front or belly side of the body.

Anthropology: The science of the origin, culture, and development of humans. This can come into play when identifying skeletal remains, certain foodstuffs or items of clothing.

Arson: To intentionally cause a fire.

Asphyxia: The result of suffocation.

Aspiration: Breathing or drawing in of a substance blocking the respiratory tract blocking the tract.

Autoeroticism: Arousal and satisfaction of sexual emotion, within or by oneself through fantasy and or genital stimulation.

Autopsy: The internal examination of the body after death.

Autorad: Common term for "Autoradiograph," the final product in a DNA analysis. Autorads, which look very much like bar codes, are formed by the reaction of electricity with genetic material (DNA). This reaction is unique to each sample of genetic material, providing an invaluable tool for identification. The reaction takes place on a nylon membrane, which is photographed against x-ray film.

Avulsion: The separation, by tearing, of any part of the body from the whole.

Ballistics: The science of the motion of projectiles. When a bullet is fired, it will have distinctive characteristics caused by the gun from which it is fired. Examiners can use this evidence to match bullets or bullet fragments to specific weapons.

Biometrics: The use of the biological make-up of the human body to identify a person (fingerprints, retinal scan, facial recognition, etc…).

Blood Spatter: The impact of spilled blood on surfaces. The pattern of the impact can provide vital information about the source of the blood. Blood spatter can help determine the size and type of wounds, the direction and speed with which the perpetrator or victim was moving, and the type of weapons used to create the blood spill.

Blood Stain Interpretation: The interpretation of size, shape, orientation, and distribution of bloodstains on various surfaces, and what information can be derived from the proper interpretation of the stains.

Blunt Trauma: The impact injury on the body from being struck by an object that does not pierce the skin.

Botany: The scientific study of plants. Plant matter found at crime scenes is organic material and, like bodily fluids, has unique DNA sequences.

Break: The point where a perpetrator forced entry into a home or business. Breaks are commonly found in burglary scenes.

Bullet Track: The path of the bullet or projectile as it passes through the body.

Burking: Mechanical asphyxia plus smothering that is homicidal in nature. Murder by suffocating so as to leave the body unmarked.

Cadaveric Spasm: Stiffening and rigidity of a single group of muscles occurring immediately after death.

Caliber: The diameter of the bore of a rifled firearm, usually expressed in hundredths of an inch.

Calling Card: Something purposely left at the scene of a crime by the suspect to leave his/her mark on that crime.

Canvass: A door-to-door search for witnesses.

Cartridge: A live bullet capable of firing from a firearm.

Casing: The metal shell of a cartridge.

Cast-off-blood: Blood that travels from a source due to the movement of that source. A bleeding person will cast-off blood, as will a weapon or other item that is in movement.

Cause of Death: Any injury or disease that produces a physiological derangement in the body that results in the individual dying.

Chop Wounds: Wounds caused by a heavy object which has an edge: an axe, machete, or a meat cleaver.

Clustered Crime Scene: A crime scene situation where most of the activities take place at one location; the confrontation, the attack, the assault, and sexual activity, etc.

Composite drawing: A sketch of a suspect produced from eyewitness-descriptions of one or more persons.

Computer Forensics: The application of computer technology for the purpose of examining potential evidence, including, but not limited to: theft of trade secrets; theft of, or destruction of property; and fraud. Specialists can recover data that has been deleted, encrypted, or damaged.

Contact Wound: A wound made when the firearm is pressed against the head or body. Consequently, gases from the explosion expand between the skin and the bone producing a bursting effect and ragged wound.

Contamination: When a foreign substance is left at a crime scene or when unauthorized persons affect the integrity of the crime scene.

Contract: As in a murder contract. AKA: A hit. When someone is paid to kill another.

Contrecoup: Injury to a part of the body (usually the brain) caused by a blow to the opposite side. Occurs frequently in falls.

Corpse: The dead human body.

Corpus Delicti: The body of the crime. The facts constituting or proving a crime; material substance or foundation of a crime. The corpus delicti in a murder case is not just the body of the victim, but the fact that he has been murdered.

Crime scene staging: The attempt by a perpetrator or accomplice to alter a crime scene in order to reduce its evidentiary value.

Criminal Profiling: A tool used to aid investigators by providing information about the type of individual committing a specific crime. Information taken from the crime scene is integrated with known psychological theory and the history and background of the victim to draw up a biographical sketch of the perpetrator.

Criminology: The study of criminal activity and how it is dealt with by the law.

Culpable: Meriting blame or responsibility.

Cyanosis: Blueness of the skin, often due to cardiac malformation resulting in insufficient oxygenation of the blood.

Decomposition: The separation of compound bodies into their constituent principles, postmortem degeneration of the body. It involves two principles: autolysis and putrefaction.

Defecation: Elimination of solid waste matter from the intestines.

Defeminize: To remove a woman's breast as in defeminization.

Defense Wounds: Cuts, abrasions, and contusions on the hands, wrists, forearms, and arms which occur during a violent struggle as the victim attempts to ward off his or her attacker.

Depersonalization: The actions taken by a murderer to obscure the personal identity of the victim. Face may be beaten beyond recognition, or the face of the victim may be covered.

Depraved: Corrupt or perverted.

Disarticulation: Amputation or separation at a joint.

Diatom: A microscopic, single-cell form of marine or fresh-water algae, having siliceous cell walls. A body of water may contain many species of diatoms, but not all species of diatoms live in every body of water. Through painstaking examination, forensic scientists are able to identify the body of water wherein a given species of diatom lives.

Digital Image Processing: Computerized technology that enables digital processing and enhancement of an image.

Disembowel: To take out the bowels.

Dismemberment: Removing parts of a body.

Disinterment: Digging up a body after burial.

DNA (Deoxyribonucleic Acid): This molecule is housed in every nucleated cell of the body. Often described as the body's blueprints since they carry the genetic codes that govern the structure and function of every component of the body.

DNA Databanks: Databases, which store DNA profiles, collected from various classes of offenders. DNA from a given crime can be entered into the databank; it can then be matched with DNA profiles from other crimes, providing potential matches from previous convictions.

DNA Profiling: The process of testing to identify DNA patterns or types. In forensic science this testing is used to indicate parentage or to exclude or include individuals as possible sources of bodily fluid stains (blood, saliva, semen) and other biological evidence (bones, hair, teeth).

Drive-by: As in drive-by shooting. When a perpetrator shoots at the victim from a moving car. This method is common among street gangs.

Drowning: Asphyxiation because of submersion in a liquid. Sequence of events is breath holding, involuntary inspiration and gasping for air at the breaking point, loss of consciousness, and death.

Entomology: The branch of science which deals with the study of insects. For example, in making a determination of "time-of-death" a forensic entomologist evaluates the structures and habits of certain necropagous insects collected from the carrion, which provide cycle time frames for the species.

Entry wound: The wound created when a projectile enters the body.

Epidermis: The outermost layer of the skin.

Eroticism: Sexual or erotic quality or character of something.

Evidence: Anything that has been used, left, removed, altered, or contaminated during the commission of a crime.

Exhume: The disinterring or removal of a body from the grave.

Exit wound: The wound created when a projectile exits the body.

Exsanguination: Removal of blood.

Facial reconstruction: The forensic reconstruction of skeletal remains to aid facial identification.

Fatal injury: An injury resulting in death.

Fetish: Any object or nongenital part of the body that causes a habitual erotic response or fixation.

Fetus: The unborn offspring of a human or animal.

Filicide: The act of murdering one's child.

Fingerprint: The unique patterns created by skin ridges found on the palm sides of fingers and thumbs.

Floater: A dead body in the water, which comes to the surface due to decompositional gases.

Forensic Animation: The use of video technology to recreate crime scenes. Forensic animations are sometimes entered into evidence so jurors can view a sequence of events that otherwise could only be described by opposing attorneys. Some courts will not admit forensic animation into trial.

Forensic Meteorology: The study of weather patterns and how they relate to the investigation of crimes.

Forensic Pathology: The study of how and why people die; a sub-specialty of pathology.

Forensic Psychologist: A trained mental health professional who examines suspects, perpetrators and victims in order to establish their psychological state and their ability to participate in the legal process.

Forensic Science: The application of science to law and the investigation of criminal activity.

Forensic Sculpting: The attempt by a sculptor to create a likeness of a given individual using his or her skull.

Fratricide: The act of killing one's brother or sister.

Frotteurism: A sexual attraction to touching or rubbing against a nonconsenting person. Rubbing his genitals against the body of another.

Frye rule: A legal standard of admissibility used by a number of jurisdictions, which requires that scientific evidence to be introduced into court, must have gained general acceptance by the scientific community. Based on Supreme Court decision Frye v. U.S., F 1013 at 1014 (D.C. Cir. 1923). A number of these Frye rulings have occurred as a result of DNA technology. Most courts have upheld DNA.

Gas Chromograph: A forensic tool used to identify the chemical makeup of substances used in the commission of crimes. The questioned substance is burned at high temperatures. The temperature at which this material becomes gas is then charted to determine its makeup.

Genetic Fingerprinting: The use of DNA technology to identify given individuals.

Genitalia: The sexual organs. In males, the testes and penis; in female, the vulva and vagina.

Geographic Profiling: A method to help investigators locate serial offenders. The sites and times of serial crimes in a given jurisdiction are entered into a computer program. This program then processes the information to give investigators a hypothetical area in which the perpetrator lives and operates.

Glycoprotein: A semen-specific glycoprotein (P30) of prostatic origin discovered in 1978. This substance is only present in semen and has essentially replaced analysis for acid phosphatase in rape investigations except for rapid screening tests.

Graffiti: Writing on a wall or item foreign to that item, usually scrawled by a gang member.

Histotoxic: Poisonous to tissue or tissues.

Hit: See Murder Contract.

Homicidomania: Impulsive desire to commit murder.

Hyperthermia: A much higher than normal body temperature.

Hypothermia: An abnormal and dangerous condition in which the body is below 95 degrees F. Usually caused by prolonged exposure to cold.

Hypoxia: Partial deprivation of oxygen.

Incision: A wound inflicted by an instrument with a sharp cutting edge.

Incised Wound: Caused by a sharp instrument or weapon. A wound which is longer than deep, with minimum bruising, no bridging of skin, and bleeds freely.

Infanticide: The act of killing an infant soon after birth.

Laceration: A split or tear of the skin, usually produced by blunt force (shearing or crushing type injuries from blunt objects, falls, or impact of vehicles). These injuries tend to be irregular with abraded contused margins. Internal organs can also have locations.

Latent Fingerprint: A fingerprint made by deposits of oils and/or perspiration, not usually visible to the human eye. Various technologies, including lasers, can be used to identify latent prints.

Lie Detector: Also known as a "Polygraph." A machine that charts how respiration and other bodily functions change as questions are asked of the person being tested. An attempt to knowingly provide false answers can cause changes in bodily functions. Lie detector tests are not admissible in court.

Ligature: Anything which binds or ties.

Linkage: The link between the crime scene, the victim, physical evidence and the suspect. It is also referred to as The Theory of Transfer and Exchange.

Linkage Blindness: An investigative failure to recognize a pattern which "links" one crime with another crime in a series of cases through victimology, geographic region or area of events, the "signature" of the offender, similar M.O., and a review of autopsy protocols.

Lividity: Also known as "liver mortis." Postmortem discoloration caused by the gravitation of blood to various parts of the body. Can be used to help determine time of death, and placement of a body after death.

Livor Mortis: Postmortem discoloration due to the gravitation of blood into the dependent capillaries and veins.

Luminol: A chemical that is capable of detecting bloodstains diluted up to 10,000 times. Luminol is used to identify blood that has been removed from a given area. It is an invaluable tool for investigators at altered crime scenes.

Manner of Death: Explains how the cause of death came about. Medico legal manners of death are: homicide, suicide, accident, natural, and undetermined.

Masochism: Sexual perversion in which the individual takes delight in being subject to degrading, humiliating, or cruel treatment such as flogging or chocking.

M.E. (Medical Examiner): A medical doctor who determines causes of death, performs autopsies, and acts as an expert witness in criminal and civil trials where cause and/or manner of death are relevant.

Mechanical Asphyxia: Asphyxia created by pressure on the outside of the body, which prevents respiration. Examples are: traumatic asphyxia, positional asphyxia, and riot crush or "human pile" deaths.

Mechanism of Death: The physiological derangement produced by the cause of death that results in death, i.e., hemorrhage, septicemia, cardiac arrhythmia.

Micro-spectro Photometry: The use of an electronic microscope in which electrons are beamed onto the specimen. The analyst then charts the electron emissions that are created in order to identify the specimen.

Mitochondrial DNA: A short sequence found outside of the cell nucleus in cells. Called mitochondria, this material is used in the absence of quality genetic material like blood, semen or saliva. It is passed only from mother to child;

siblings share maternal mitochondria. Hairs and fingernails are good sources of mitochondria.

Modus Operandi: "Mode of Operation" or way of doing things. The M.O. is a learned behavior that changes as offenders gain experience, build confidence, or become involved with the criminal justice system.

Mummification: The complete drying up of the body as the result of burial in a dry place, or by exposure to dry atmosphere.

Necrophagia: The eating of dead bodies or feeding off a carrion, e.g., necrophagous insects such as flies and beetles can provide entomological evidence in death investigations.

Necrophilism: Morbid attraction to corpses; sexual intercourse with a dead body.

Neonaticide: The killing of a child within 24 hours of its birth.

Odontology: The study of the anatomy, growth, and diseases of the teeth. In the absence of other factors, odontology can be used to identify human remains.

Orthotolodine Solution: A chemical solution that will determine whether a given stain contains blood.

Ouchterlony Test: A test that determines if a blood stain is human or animal.

Overlay: Mechanical asphyxia combined with smothering. An example would be an infant in bed with one of the parents, who inadvertently rolls on top of the child, thus compressing the chest and occluding the nose and mouth with the bedding or the body.

Padding: Material placed between a body portion and the ligature or device used to alter the physiological state of the victim.

Parenticide: The act of killing one's own parents.

Pathology: The study of the essential nature of diseases and especially of the structural and functional changes produced by them.

Pedophilia: Engaging in sexual activity with prepubertal children. Pedophile – A person who engages in pedophilia.

Perpology: The study and in-depth investigation of the perpetrator/suspect of a crime which includes criminal history, M.O., associates and pending cases.

Perspective Analysis: In order to determine the size of objects within a given photograph, analysts will identify one item in that photograph and measure the distance between that item and the camera used to make the photograph. This perspective allows them to measure everything in the photograph.

Physical Evidence: Any object that can establish that a crime has been committed, or can provide a link between a crime and its victim, or between a crime and its perpetrator.

Physiological Mechanism: The ligature or device used to alter the physiological state of the victim.

Piquerism: Sexual inclinations to stab, pierce, or cut. Obtaining a sexual gratification from the shedding of blood, tearing of flesh, and/or observing such pain and suffering of a victim who is being subjected to this activity.

Positional Asphyxia: Asphyxia which occurs as a result of body position, which restricts respiration.

Posterior: (Dorsal) Indicates the backside of the body. Hence, the heels are posterior or dorsal.

Postmortem: After death.

Postpartum: Pertaining to the period following childbirth.

Primary Officer: The first officer responsible for the crime scene until the investigator responds.

Probable Cause: Reasonable grounds to believe that a person has committed a crime.

Projectile: An object or shrapnel fired from a device (firearm, bow, explosive, etc).

Psychodynamics: The study of the mental and emotional processes underlying human behavior and its motivation.

Psychological Profile: A tool used to aid investigators by providing speculative information about a perpetrator's psychological makeup. Information from crime scenes is integrated with psychological theory and then cross-referenced against similar crimes. The result is a hypothetical model of the suspect that can include age, occupation, appearance, and personal information ranging from sexual preferences to dietary habits.

Psychopathic Personality: A person whose behavior is largely amoral and asocial and who is characterized by irresponsibility, lack of remorse or shame, perverse or impulsive (often criminal) behavior, and other serious personality defects, generally without psychotic attacks or symptoms.

Psychosis: A major mental disorder in which the personality is very seriously disorganized and contact with reality is impaired.

Psychotic: Of or having the nature of a psychosis; having a psychosis – a person who has a psychosis.

Pugilistic Attitude: Position the body assumes in fire deaths. Coagulation of the muscle due to heat causes contraction of muscle fibers with resultant flexion of the limbs.

Puncture Wound: A wound that is neither an impact wound nor one caused by a projectile; a piercing of the body, usually by a handheld object.

Purge Fluid: Decomposition fluid which drains from the mouth or nose. Sometimes mistaken as blood and head trauma.

Putrefaction: Decomposition of soft tissues by bacteria and fermentation and enzymes. After death, the bacteria flora of the gastrointestinal tract invades the vascular system, spreading throughout the body, producing putrefaction.

Questioned Documents: Any object that contains handwritten or typewritten markings whose source or authenticity are not known, but which is still relevant to the outcome of a legal proceeding.

Rape Kit: Biological material collected from a rape victim after the fact, to obtain genetic material of the suspected perpetrator.

Remains: That which is left over after a long period of time of a human body or animal.

Resuscitation: To revive, as in drowning or electrical shock.

Ridge Characteristics: Ridge endings, bifurcations, enclosures, and other ridge details, which must match in two fingerprints for their common origin to be established.

Rigor Mortis: A rigidity or stiffening of the muscular tissue and joints of the body after death due to the disappearance of adenosine triphosphate (ATP) from muscle.

Sadism: Getting sexual pleasure from dominating, mistreating, or hurting one's partner. Obtaining sexual gratification from inflicting physical or psychological pain on another.

Schizophrenia: A major mental disorder of unknown cause typically characterized by separation between thought processes and the emotions; a distortion of reality accompanied by delusions and hallucinations; a fragmentation of the personality, motor disturbances, bizarre behavior, etc., often with no loss of basic intellectual functions.

Secretor: An individual who secretes his or her blood-type antigen(s) in bodily fluids. Before DNA technology, blood type from bodily fluids other than blood could only be obtained from secretors, who make up about 80 percent of the population.

Self-rescue Mechanism: The object (knife, key) or method (pressure point change) utilized by the victim to alleviate the effects of the physiological mechanism.

Serial Murder: Three or more consecutive murders.

Serology: The science dealing with the properties and actions of serums, e.g., blood analysis.

SIDS: SIDS is an acronym for Sudden Infant Death Syndrome, AKA Crib death, as characterized by the sudden, unexpected death of an apparently healthy infant.

Signature: Signature is the aspect of a series of crimes leading the investigators to believe the crimes were committed by the same person.

Slashing: Common assault technique used by gang members where a cutting instrument slashes the skin causing a large laceration.

Smothering: Asphyxia due to mechanical obstruction or occlusion of the external airways, e.g., mouth and nose.

Spectrograph: A technology that measures how a given object responds to frequencies within the light spectrum. Objects can be identified and their properties visually clarified by use of this technology.

Spree Murder: The murder of more than one person at two or more locations during a single event without any cooling-off period

Stab Wounds: Caused by relatively sharp, pointed instruments such as knives, screwdrivers, ice picks, daggers, scissors, or pieces of glass. These wounds are deeper than they are wide, with possible damage to vital organs beneath the skin and bone, and internal bleeding, with little or no external blood.

Staged: Occurs when a perpetrator purposely alters the crime to mislead the authorities or redirect the investigation.

Stippling: Also referred to as Tattooing, which are pinpoint hemorrhages due to the discharge of burning powder against the skin.

Strangulation: Any abnormal constriction of the throat, causing a suspension of breathing.

Subdural Hematoma: The most common lethal injury associated with head trauma. Bleeding, almost always from injury, between the inside of the skull and the dura which covers the brain. This accumulation of blood produces pressure on the brain.

Suffocation: The failure of oxygen to reach the blood. This can occur through entrapment, smothering, choking, mechanical asphyxia combined with smothering, or through suffocating gases.

Super Glue Fuming: Techniques used to develop latent fingerprints on non-porous surfaces. A chemical in the glue reacts with and adheres to the finger oils, and then expose latent prints.

Suspension Point: The location from which the victim has suspended himself.

Survival Interval: The period of time between the infliction of injury and the actual death.

Tache Noir: It is an artifact of the drying eye after death, consisting of a brown to black band of discolored sclera where the eyes are partly open and exposed to the air.

Tagging: As in graffiti. Some gang members will tag their gang's name or their nickname at the scene of a crime.

Tattooing: Pinpoint hemorrhages on the skin caused by the discharge of burned gunpowder.

Telephone Scatologia: A sexual attraction to making obscene telephone calls (lewdness).

Theory of Transfer and Exchange: The link between the crime scene, the victim, physical evidence and the suspect. It is also referred to as linkage.

Torso: The trunk of the body without the head or extremities.

Toxic: Poisonous.

Toxicology: The scientific study of poisons, their detection, their effects, and methods of treatment for conditions they produce.

Trajectory: The path of a projectile.

Trace Evidence: Material deposited at a crime scene that can only be detected through a deliberate processing procedure. An individual entering any environment will deposit traces of his or her presence, and this material can be used as evidence. Common sources of trace evidence are hairs and fibers.

Trauma: A physical injury caused by a violent or disruptive action, or by the introduction into the body of a toxic substance.

Urolangia: A sexual desire to consume urine.

Victimology: Pedigree such as sex, age, height, weight, etc. The essential information about the victim, such as family, friends and acquaintances, education, employment, residence, neighborhood, etc. This also includes the background information on the lifestyle of the victim. Was this person a low, moderate, or high-risk victim?

Wadding: The material used to pad a shotgun shell from a lead projectile, buck shot or bird shot.

Suggested Tools for Crime Scene Investigation

An investigator never knows what a crime scene will encompass, nor will he/she ever be able to predict what type of evidence will be collected. It is important to be prepared for anything that may arise.

Here is a suggested list of supplies and tools to put in the investigator's crime scene kit:

1. Camera
2. Cassette recorder (mini)
3. Chalk
4. Clipboard
5. Cotton gloves
6. Cotton swabs
7. Coveralls
8. Crime scene tape
9. Door seal (crime scene)
10. Evidence packages
11. Evidence tags
12. Extension cord
13. Fingerprint kit
14. Flashlight
15. Forceps

16. Graph paper
17. Hammer and Nails
18. Luminol
19. Magnifying Glass
20. Marking Crayons
21. Mask (surgical)
22. Masking Tape
23. Note Pad
24. Paper bags
25. Plastic zip-lock bags
26. Polaroid Camera
27. Rope (at least 100 ft)
28. Ruler
29. Scissors
30. Screwdriver (multi-tip)
31. Shovel/Spade (collapsible)
32. Street directory/map
33. Surgical gloves
34. Tape measure
35. Thermometer
36. Tweezers
37. Video camera (if available)
38. Wipes (hand)

NOTES

NOTES

NOTES

NOTES

Path of the Warrior
An Ethical Guide to Personal & Professional Development in the Field of Criminal Justice
by Larry F. Jetmore

The COMPSTAT Paradigm
Management Accountability in Policing, Business and the Public Sector
by Vincent E. Henry, CPP, Ph.D.

The New Age of Police Supervision and Management
A Behavioral Concept
by Michael A. Petrillo & Daniel R. DelBagno

Effective Police Leadership
Moving Beyond Management
by Thomas E. Baker, Lt. Col. MP USAR (Ret.)

(800) 647-5547
www.LooseleafLaw.com

**Also provided by
CTS Associates Incorporated:**

PRODUCTS

The Pocketguide Series published by Looseleaf Law

SERVICES

Protective Services
Private Investigation

TRAINING COURSES

Basic Gang Identification Course
Gang Interdiction Course (LEO)
Street Smarts: A Crime Prevention Course
Interview and Interrogation
Hostage Negotiation Course
Dignitary and Executive Protection Course
Language Immersion Courses

…plus many more courses available

UPCOMING SEMINARS

Dealing with Gangs Effectively: The Seminar
Terrorism: *The threat in the US*

 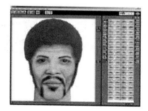

One should always look for a possible alternative and provide against it. It is the first rule of criminal investigation.

Sherlock Holmes